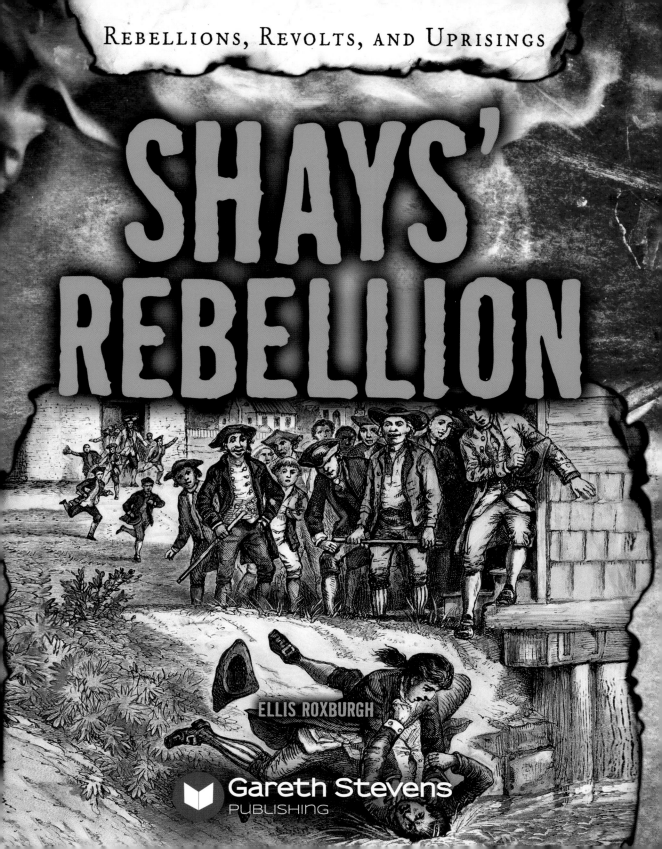

SHAYS' REBELLION

ELLIS ROXBURGH

Gareth Stevens
PUBLISHING

Please visit our website, www.garethstevens.com. For a free color catalog of all our high-quality books, call toll-free 1-800-542-2595 or fax 1-877-542-2596.

CATALOGING-IN-PUBLICATION DATA

Names: Roxburgh, Ellis.
Title: Shays Rebellion / Ellis Roxburgh.
Description: New York : Gareth Stevens Publishing, 2018. | Series: Rebellions, revolts, and uprisings | Includes index.
Identifiers: ISBN 9781538207727 (pbk.) | ISBN 9781538207680 (library bound) | ISBN 9781538207567 (6 pack)
Subjects: LCSH: Shays' Rebellion, 1786-1787--Juvenile literature.
Classification: LCC F69.R69 2018 | DDC 974.4'03--dc23

Published in 2018 by
Gareth Stevens Publishing
111 East 14th Street, Suite 349
New York, NY 10003

Copyright © 2018 Gareth Stevens

For Brown Bear Books Ltd:
Managing Editor: Tim Cooke
Designer: Lynne Lennon
Editorial Director: Lindsey Lowe
Children's Publisher: Anne O'Daly
Design Manager: Keith Davis
Picture Manager: Sophie Mortimer

Picture Credits: Cover: Getty: Bettmann.nterior: Alamy: Granger Hisorical Picture Archive 26; Granger Collection: 31; istockphoto: 14; Library of Congress: 4, 5, 7, 8, 9, 15, 18, 19, 20, 21, 28, 29, 32, 36, 37, 38, 42; NARA: 16; Public Domain: 39, John Bessa 34, National Portrait Gallery, Washington 13, New York Public Library 12, Private Collection 30, statuepeeper 23, Antoine Taveneaux 41, United States Capitol 43; Shutterstock: Mary Lane 27, Nagel Photography 25; Smithsonian Institution: National Museum of American History 11, 22; Thinkstock: istockphoto 6, 10, 40; Topfoto: The Granger Collection 17, 24, 33; Yale University: Beinecke Rare Book Library 35.

All other artworks and maps Brown Bear Books

Brown Bear Books has made every attempt to contact the copyright holder.
If anyone has any information please contact licensing@brownbearbooks.co.uk

Manufactured in the United States of America

CPSIA compliance information: Batch #CS17GS. For further information contact Gareth Stevens, New York, New York at 1-800-542-2595.

CONTENTS

Roots of Rebellion 4

Who Were the Rebels? 12

Rebellion! 20

Fighting Authority 28

Defeat and Legacy 36

Timeline 44

Glossary 46

Further Information 47

Index 48

WORDS IN THE GLOSSARY APPEAR IN **BOLD** TYPE
THE FIRST TIME THEY ARE USED IN THE TEXT.

ROOTS OF REBELLION

Just 3 years after the Revolutionary War ended in 1783, thousands of citizens from the new state of Massachusetts rose up in a violent rebellion against the new US government.

The rebellion that shook Massachusetts in 1786 and 1787 had its roots in the aftermath of the Revolutionary War (1775–1783). On July 4, 1776, the 13 **colonies** had declared indepedence from their colonial ruler, Great Britain.

The British surrender at the Battle of Yorktown in 1781, ending the fighting in the Revolutionary War.

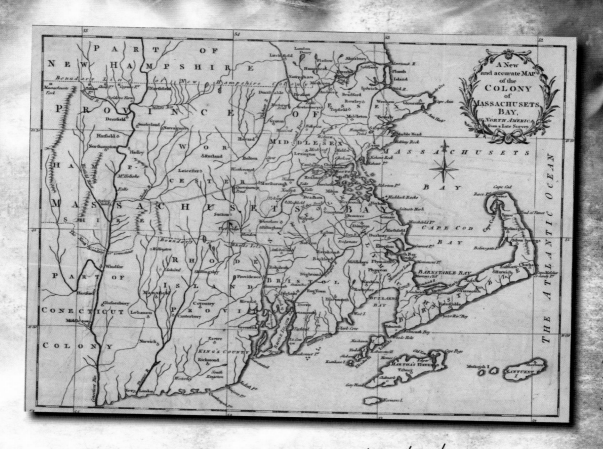

This map shows Massachusetts before independence. The state was divided between heavily populated regions in the East and remote, rural regions in the West.

It took until 1783 for the Continental Army to secure American independence by defeating the British. The war had been expensive, and victory left the former colonies **bankrupt** and facing huge debt. Many soldiers in the Continental Army were owed **back salaries**, which needed to be paid before the army was disbanded. The government made temporary loans to the different colonies to help with payments, but they still faced huge debt. A combination of reasons meant that the situation hit Massachusetts particularly hard.

COLONY ON EDGE

MASSACHUSETTS HAD A HISTORY OF REBELLION AGAINST AUTHORITY. IN 1773, BOSTONIANS THREW BRITISH TEA INTO BOSTON HARBOR AS A PROTEST AGAINST BRITISH TAXES. IN 1774, 1,500 MEN SURROUNDED THE COURTHOUSE IN SPRINGFIELD TO PROTEST THE BRITISH PARLIAMENT ACT. THE ACT TOOK POWER AWAY FROM THE COLONISTS AND GAVE IT TO A ROYAL GOVERNOR. THESE EVENTS WERE AMONG A SERIES OF PROTESTS THAT EVENTUALLY LED TO THE OUTBREAK OF WAR.

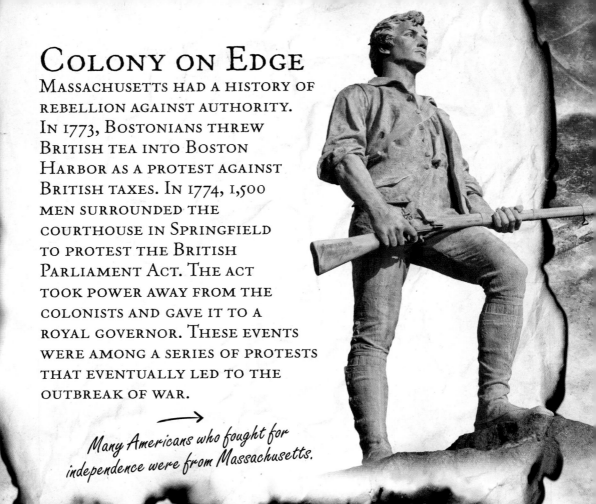

Many Americans who fought for independence were from Massachusetts.

A Postwar Boom

The end of the Revolutionary War brought a short-lived **boom** as Americans rushed to buy **imported** goods that had not been available during the war. British factories were manufacturing cheap items such as furniture and, despite having lost their colonies, the British were happy to trade with the United States. Ship after ship docked in US ports with cheap goods to sell. However, the British Navy stopped American trade with Britain's colonies in the Caribbean. US national income fell dramatically. In November 1783, the United States was plunged into a severe **recession**.

In order to pay for the war, the US government had printed paper money. With the recession, that money had lost its value, causing a rise in prices known as **inflation**. Some Americans feared that the new **republic** would not survive.

The Recession Worsens

Conditions grew steadily worse. By the fall of 1784, the country was in economic crisis. Many individuals faced huge debts, and paid less in taxes. Neither individuals, states, nor the federal government could pay their bills.

In Massachusetts, the state government imposed new taxes. It also ordered its citizens to pay their outstanding debts.

The economic crisis badly hit trade at Massachusetts ports such as Salem.

THE ARTICLES OF CONFEDERATION

IN 1777, THE LEADERS OF THE 13 AMERICAN COLONIES CREATED A BLUEPRINT FOR HOW THE NEW UNITED STATES WOULD BE GOVERNED. THE ARTICLES OF CONFEDERATION WAS THE WORLD'S FIRST WRITTEN CONSTITUTION. ITS WRITERS INTENDED TO SHOW THAT GOOD GOVERNMENT COULD BE PLANNED RATHER THAN COMING ABOUT BY CHANCE.

→

The Articles of Confederation was the first written US constitution.

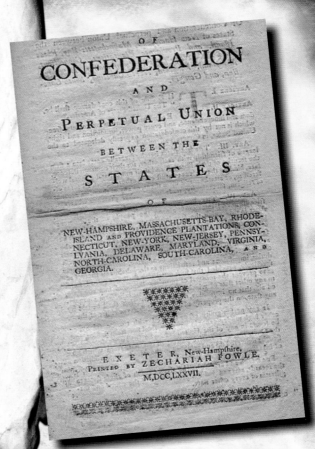

Some of the people with the greatest debt were farmers who had to buy seed and equipment before they could produce a crop for sale. Other states passed laws to help **debtors**, but Massachsetts did not. In addition, it ordered that debts and taxes must be paid in gold and silver coins, or "hard currency." Most citizens of Massachusetts had no gold or silver. They usually settled debts with goods, such as timber or grain.

A Change of Governor

The governor of Massachusetts, John Hancock, understood the problems of poor farmers. He refused to enforce the law that debts had to be paid in hard currency.

That did not prevent growing unrest among the farmers of central and western Massachusetts. Meanwhile, merchants and manufacturers who were owed money were eager for the debt laws to be enforced. In 1785, Hancock was replaced by James Bowdoin, who insisted that all taxes should be paid in hard currency, no matter how poor the debtor. Soon the courts were full of lawsuits for unpaid debts.

A Weak Government

The crisis in Massachusetts revealed a fundamental problem. During the Revolutionary War, the 13 colonies had set out to create a national government.

John Hancock, later the governor of Massachusetts, had been the first man to sign the Declaration of Independence in 1776.

Exchange Economy

The farmers of western Massachusetts operated what is known as an exchange economy. When they needed something, the farmers swapped their own products or time for the goods. This process was called barter. No money exchanged hands. People usually settled debts in the same way. Even stores and other businesses allowed customers to use barter to pay for goods or services.

Timber was one of the most commonly bartered resources in western Massachusetts.

The colonies were anxious not to copy the government of their former rulers in Great Britain. When the revolutionary leaders drew up the Articles of Confederation—the first constitution of the United States—they gave only limited powers to the new national government.

Critics of this constitution argued that it would cause problems. The US Congress had only limited powers to make treaties and **alliances** with foreign powers, to coin money, and to keep an army. There was no **centralized** organization to raise taxes or control business.

Financial control was the responsibility of each state. Congress only became involved in such issues as a last resort if a state was unable to sort out its own problems. Now it was clear that Massachusetts was failing to raise taxes or control business. Bowdoin's intention of bringing state finances under control was not working, because many citizens simply had no means of paying their debts or taxes, which were now higher than they had been under British rule.

This banknote was printed in Massachusetts in 1741. At the time, each colony had its own currency, based on the British pound.

WHO WERE THE REBELS?

The Massachusetts rebellions of 1786 and 1787 were named after Daniel Shays, but he was not the only leader of the uprisings.

By the summer of 1786, farmers and **smallholders** in western Massachusetts had started to rebel against the punishing new tax **regime** the state had introduced. Not only were the new taxes higher than under British rule, but veterans of the Revolutionary War were also being asked to clear their debts when they had not yet been paid for their war efforts. Massachusetts' businessmen were trying to get customers to pay the money they were owed so that they could pay back their own debts to their suppliers, who were sometimes based in Europe.

Governor James Bowdoin was sympathetic to the demands of Massachusetts businessmen.

This drawing of the time shows two leading rebels, Daniel Shays (left) and Job Shattuck.

To make things worse for the farmers, veterans, and smallholders, Governor Bowdoin supported the demands of these businessmen for payment in hard currency. In 1786, two veterans of the Continental Army and a Massachusetts landowner rallied their fellow citizens to fight back.

Daniel Shays

Daniel Shays (1747–1825) was a veteran of the Revolutionary War. He had fought in the Battles of Lexington (1775) and Saratoga (1777) and had reached the rank of captain before he resigned from the army in 1780.

On his return home to Massachusetts, Shays was taken to court for unpaid debts. He could not pay because he had not been paid for his military service. Shays soon discovered that many other veterans were in the same position.

Paper Money

During the Revolutionary War, the United States issued its own banknotes, known as Continental Currency. By 1780, however, these bills were worth just 2.5 percent of their face value thanks to inflation, or a general rise in prices. As a result, the Massachusetts government only accepted gold and silver coins as money. However, during the financial crisis, it became too expensive to mint more coins, so some people were eager that the state start to accept paper money.

→

From 1836 to 1865, private banks in the United States could print their own paper money.

While John Hancock was governor, Shays and other men protested the unfairness of the tax and debt demands by writing to the state government in Boston. Although they sent **petitions** and proposals to solve the problem, the state rejected all their suggestions. One of Shays' suggestions was that Massachusetts should issue more paper money to help the farmers pay off their debts, rather than insisting on hard currency. Shays and his supporters argued that this had been done in other states. The Massachusetts government refused.

Shays Leads the Rebels

When James Bowdoin became governor in May 1785, it soon became clear that he was determined to collect all debts. The following summer, Shays and his fellow protestors decided they had no choice but to take direct action. On August 29, 1786, they marched to Northampton to stop the court from sitting and issuing more fines for debts. Shays also organized protests at other county court hearings to stop the work of the debt collectors across the state.

Shays had fought in the Battle of Lexington in 1775. ↓

A British army general (red coat) surrenders at the Battle of Saratoga in 1777. Luke Day fought in the American victory.

Luke Day

Like Daniel Shays, Luke Day (1743–1801) was another veteran of the Revolutionary War, but the two men had very different backgrounds. While Shays was a poor farmer, Day was a gentleman who came from one of the leading families in West Springfield. As a soldier, Day had fought in many of the key battles of the war, including the Siege of Boston (1775–1776) and the Battle of Saratoga. He was also promoted to captain.

While on leave from the war in 1782, Day helped put down a rebellion against the Massachusetts wartime government. He defended judges at county courts against an uprising. Day's position changed after the war, when his own family fell on hard times. Like many other families in Massachusetts, the Days found themselves in debt.

THE REGULATORS

THE REBELS CALLED THEMSELVES "REGULATORS." THEY TOOK THE NAME FROM A POPULAR MOVEMENT IN NORTH CAROLINA IN THE 1760S. THE NORTH CAROLINA REGULATORS WERE FARMERS WHO HAD OPPOSED THE TAXATION SYSTEM AND CORRUPTION OF THE COLONIAL GOVERNMENT. THE CAROLINA REGULATORS ATTACKED SETTLERS. IN 1768, THEY DISRUPTED THE COLONIAL COURT AT HILLSBOROUGH. IN 1771, 2,000 REGULATORS HAD FOUGHT THE COLONIAL MILITIA AT ALAMANCE AND WERE EASILY DEFEATED.

Day played a key role in Shays' Rebellion. He led protests at courts, drilled the militia, and planned strategy with Shays. Some historians think the rebels chose Shays as leader because Day was too **excitable**. Day's part in the rebellion angered his family. They **disowned** him, and he was later buried in an unmarked grave.

Job Shattuck

The third leader of the rebellion was the biggest landowner in Groton, in northwest Massachusetts. Job Shattuck (1736–1819) had a fine military career.

A tax collector demands payment from a blacksmith in Massachusetts.

Shattuck had served in the Revolutionary War, becoming a captain in the Massachusetts State

Most of the rebels had fought British Redcoats in the Revolutionary War.

Militia. Shattuck was 50 years old and a well-respected member of the community when he joined the rebels, who called themselves "Regulators." As a landowner, Shattuck objected to what he saw as unreasonable financial demands of the state and an attack on his personal liberties. Shattuck would lead a group of rebels that shut down the state courthouse in Concord in September 1786. He set up a Regulator camp there, which easily outnumbered the government supporters.

THE GROTON RIOTS

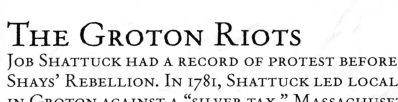

Job Shattuck had a record of protest before Shays' Rebellion. In 1781, Shattuck led local people in Groton against a "silver tax." Massachusetts had refused to allow townsfolk to pay taxes in paper money, demanding gold or silver. Shattuck led rioters who prevented the town constable from collecting the taxes. In April 1782, Shattuck was found guilty of rioting and ordered to pay a fine of £10.

Groton was a small town in northwestern Massachusetts. ↓

REBELLION!

During the summer of 1786, the Regulators were able to prevent court proceedings taking place against debt-ridden farmers in several different towns in Massachusetts.

After the Regulators had succeeded in preventing the court in Northampton, Massachusetts, from opening on August 29, 1786, Governor Bowdoin decided to act. On September 2, he issued a **proclamation** denouncing the Regulators as a "mob." He decided to use the state militia to respond to future action by the Regulators.

When the Regulators shut down the court in Worcester County on September 5, Bowdoin ordered the local militia to act. They refused to turn out against the Regulators.

→

This is the modern courthouse in Northampton, Massachusetts.

Most of the militia in Worcester County supported the actions of the protesters. Instead, the Supreme Court of Massachusetts **indicted** 11 leaders of the revolt on September 19. The stage was set for confrontation.

A Clash

On September 26, 1786, the state government called for volunteers to rush to Springfield, Massachusetts, to join a hastily gathered militia to defend the courthouse. The government wanted to protect the supreme judicial court, which was due to sit that day. Everyone expected the Regulators to try and stop the court from opening.

A veteran of the Continental Army, General William Shepard, took command of the 300 or so men who joined the state militia. Shepard armed them and placed two cannons in front of the courthouse. Daniel Shays and Luke Day led a similar number of Regulators. They were armed with muskets, swords, and clubs.

OTHER STATES

MASSACHUSETTS WAS NOT THE ONLY STATE TO FACE PROTESTS ABOUT HARSH TAXATION AND DEBT COLLECTION. IN OTHER STATES, STATE GOVERNMENTS SENT THE LOCAL MILITIA TO PUT DOWN ANY REBELLION AT THE FIRST SIGN OF PROTEST. IN RHODE ISLAND, HOWEVER, THE GOVERNMENT SUPPORTED THE REBELS. MERCHANTS IN THE STATE WERE FORCED TO ACCEPT THE DEVALUED PAPER CURRENCY.

Rhode Island forced merchants to accept banknotes, like this one, printed in the state in 1780.

People gathered to watch the confrontation at the courthouse. Some joined the Regulators, while others joined the militia. By the time the confrontation came to an end, the militia had been increased in number to around 800 men. The Regulators numbered 1,200. The court opened for business as normal, but the judges soon found that it was impossible to hear any proceedings because of all the shouting and noise coming from the two rival groups outside.

A Temporary Truce

With men on both sides marching and chanting, Shays spoke to General Shepard. He asked for the court to remain shut until peoples' **grievances** had been addressed. He also asked the government to dismiss the militia. Shepard refused to agree to either request, but he agreed that the Regulators could continue to march peacefully around the courthouse.

The Regulators marched around the courthouse for 2 tense days, until the court accepted that it would not be able to carry out any business and adjourned. Shepard ordered the militia to withdraw to the federal **armory**, which he feared might be attacked. When no attack came, Shepard sent his men home.

The Regulators then briefly occupied the courthouse. It was a purely **symbolic** act, because the courthouse was now empty. After that, the Regulators disbanded and headed for home.

→

This statue of William Shepard stands in his hometown, Westfield, Massachusetts.

This illustration shows the Regulators after their occupation of the courthouse at Springfield.

Protests Continue

Protests continued through October 1786. Courts across Massachusetts could only sit with militia protection. To try to stop the protests, the Massachusetts state government passed a Riot Act to prevent people gathering and suspended **habeas corpus**, which protected people from unlawful arrest. The state government also made concessions, allowing some debts to be paid with goods rather than hard currency. The new laws did not stop the protests, however.

Arrest of Job Shattuck

Matters came to a head again at the end of November 1786.

Court business across the state was suspended by the threat from the Regulators.

Politicians in Boston regarded Job Shattuck as being one of the **ringleaders** of the protests. Around 300 men were sent to Groton to arrest him. After spending 2 days on the run, Shattuck was finally captured. His captors slashed him with a sword during the arrest, nearly severing his leg.

DID YOU KNOW?

HABEAS CORPUS BEGAN IN THE 1300s IN ENGLAND. IT PROTECTED PEOPLE FROM ARREST BY MAKING JAILERS PROVE THAT ALL ARRESTS WERE LEGAL.

THE RIOT ACT

THE RIOT ACT WAS PASSED IN FALL 1786 IN MASSACHUSETTS AS A DIRECT RESPONSE TO SHAYS' REBELLION. THE ACT'S TERMS WERE BASED ON A BRITISH RIOT ACT OF 1714. THEY STATED THAT GATHERINGS OF 12 OR MORE PEOPLE COULD BE DECLARED UNLAWFUL AND FORCED TO BREAK UP. THE MASSACHUSETTS ACT ENTITLED LAW OFFICIALS AND THE MILITIA TO USE FORCE IF PEOPLE REFUSED TO OBEY AN ORDER TO DISPERSE. PROTESTERS COULD EVEN BE KILLED.

Massachusetts militia open fire on protesters during Shays' Rebellion. The rebellion led to the passing of the Riot Act.

The rebels aimed to overthrow the government in the Massachusetts State House in Boston.

As word of Shattuck's arrest spread, the Regulators decided to take more drastic action. Their protests had been largely ignored. Shays, Day, and others decided they would overthrow the Massachusetts government. The Regulators started to consider how to put their plan into effect.

When the Massachusetts government learned what was being plotted, they acted. The state did not have enough money to raise an army. Instead, Governor Bowdoin suggested that the rich merchants and landowners who supported his tough approach toward debtors pay to form a militia force.

FIGHTING AUTHORITY

By January 1787, Massachusetts was ready for conflict. The Regulators plotted to overthrow the government, while Governor Bowdoin urged his supporters to recruit a private army.

Bowdoin had appealed to private individuals to pay for a militia. He put a veteran of the Continental Army, General Benjamin Lincoln, in charge of raising funds to pay for this force. By the middle of January 1787, Lincoln had persuaded more than 125 merchants to donate over £6,000, which was enough to pay for 3,000 men.

→ Benjamin Lincoln served as George Washington's second-in-command in the Revolutionary War.

Benjamin Lincoln set up two cannons to defend the federal arsenal. ↑

The new militiamen almost all came from the eastern counties of Massachusetts. On January 19, 1787, they marched west to take up positions in Worcester and Springfield.

The Final Rebellion

On January 25, 1787, more than 1,200 militiamen were in position in thick snow around the federal **arsenal** in Springfield, Massachusetts. They knew the Regulators were on their way to try to seize the weapons and ammunition. General William Shepard, who had defended Springfield's courthouse the previous September, was in command.

GENERAL WILLIAM SHEPARD

WILLIAM SHEPARD (1737-1817) SERVED IN THE CONTINENTAL ARMY BEFORE JOINING THE MASSACHUSETTS MILITIA. WHEN HE SAW THE REGULATORS AT SPRINGFIELD COURTHOUSE WITH NO WEAPONS BUT STICKS AND CLUBS, HE GUESSED THAT THE REBELS WOULD ATTACK THE FEDERAL ARSENAL TO STEAL WEAPONS. HE WAS PROVED RIGHT. SHEPARD'S NEIGHBORS ARE SAID TO HAVE TURNED AGAINST HIM AFTER HE OPENED FIRE ON THE REBELS AT THE ARSENAL. THE NEIGHBORS ARE SAID TO HAVE BLINDED HIS HORSES.

Shepard was a member of the US House of Representatives from 1797 to 1803.

Acting on orders from Governor Bowdoin, Shepard armed his men with weapons from the arsenal. The arsenal was federal rather than state property, but Shepard acted without seeking permission from the US Congress. He positioned two cannons in front of the building. Late in the afternoon on January 25, 1,500 Regulators appeared, marching eight abreast as they approached the arsenal.

The Regulators' Plan

The Regulators had planned a three-pronged attack. The rebels were split into three groups: one led by Daniel Shays, another led by Luke Day, and a third led by Eli Parsons.

The plan was to attack the arsenal from three different directions. At the last minute, Day sent a message to Shays to say he would not be ready until the next day, but Shepard's men intercepted the message. The Regulators who marched to the arsenal had no idea that Day's men would not be there.

The financial crisis caused tension and violence throughout Massachusetts during the rebellion.

THE SPRINGFIELD ARSENAL

THE UNITED STATES BUILT AN ARSENAL AT SPRINGFIELD IN 1777 IN ORDER TO STORE WEAPONS. IT WAS ILLEGAL TO REMOVE WEAPONS WITHOUT PERMISSION FROM THE FEDERAL GOVERNMENT. IN 1794, THE ARSENAL BECAME THE SPRINGFIELD ARMORY, MEANING THAT IT MANUFACTURED WEAPONS RATHER THAN SIMPLY STORING THEM.

This photograph shows the buildings of the Springfield Armory in 1900.

Fatal Attack

As Shays, Parsons, and their two columns of rebels marched through the snow toward the arsenal, they could see the militiamen waiting for them. General Shepard ordered his men to fire warning shots over the heads of the approaching rebels. When the advancing men failed to stop, Shepard ordered his men to open fire with the two cannons.

DID YOU KNOW?

GEORGE WASHINGTON CHOSE SPRINGFIELD AS THE SITE FOR AN ARMORY IN 1777. THE TOWN STOOD ON THREE RIVERS AND FOUR ROADS, SO WAS EASILY ACCESSIBLE.

Daniel Shays leads his men toward the Springfield arsenal.

The cannons were loaded with grapeshot—a large number of small metal balls, or shot, that scattered over a wide area when fired. The cannons fired straight at the rebels. Four of the men were killed immediately, and another 20 were wounded. The survivors turned and fled without firing a shot. Shays' Rebellion was over before it had begun.

Rounding Up the Regulators

Shays and his men fled northward, eventually reaching the town of Amherst. Day's men also made for Amherst. The rebels then all made their way to Petersham, where they set up camp, raiding local stores for food.

When General Benjamin Lincoln learned what had happened at Springfield, he led his 3,000 militiamen in pursuit of the Regulators. Lincoln led his men on a **forced march** through a freezing snowstorm overnight on February 3–4. He surprised the rebels in their camp at Petersham. Lincoln claimed to have captured 150 rebels, but most historians think that was probably an exaggeration. Some of the leaders of the rebellion crossed the state line into New Hampshire and Vermont, where sympathetic citizens hid them.

The End of the Rebellion

Lincoln's determined pursuit of the rebels put an end to any thought of continuing the protests. The same day he arrived in Petersham, Massachusetts introduced martial law. This gave the militia wide-ranging powers to act against the rebels.

→

This monument to the rebellion stands in a field near Petersham.

LAST BATTLE OF SHAYS REBELLION WAS HERE FEB. 27. 1787

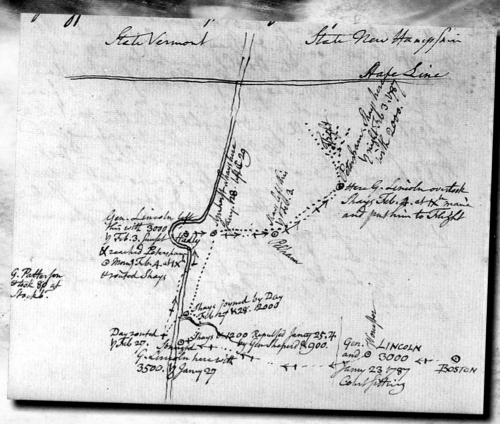

The Reverend Ezra Stiles
drew this map of the Shays' Rebellion in 1787.

The state also agreed to pay for the militia Lincoln had raised by reimbursing the merchants who had initially funded the makeshift army. The militia were sent home.

Meanwhile, the Regulators carried out one more attack. On February 27, a group of about 120 rebels returned to Massachusetts from the north. They marched to the market town of Stockbridge, where they attacked stores and the homes of merchants. A local man, Brigadier John Ashley, quickly gathered 80 men to fight the rebels. In what turned out to be the bloodiest encounter of the rebellion, one rebel and at least one of Ashley's men died and 30 rebels were wounded before the rebel assault was ended.

DEFEAT AND LEGACY

The unsuccessful rebellion had many consequences, not just for the individual Regulators but also for the state of Massachusetts and for the whole nation.

After the encounter at Petersham on February 4, 1787, 4,000 rebels handed over their weapons. In exchange for being pardoned rather than being sent to prison or hanged, they were made to swear **allegiance** to the Commonwealth of Massachusetts. A few hundred rebels were

→

This proclamation offering a reward for the capture of the rebel leaders was signed by Benjamin Franklin.

PENNSYLVANIA, ff.

By the *President* and the *Supreme Executive Council* of the Commonwealth of *Pennsylvania*,

A PROCLAMATION.

WHEREAS the General Assembly of this Commonwealth, by a law entitled 'An act for co-operating with " the state of Massachusetts bay, agreeable to the articles of " confederation, in the apprehending of the proclaimed rebels " DANIEL SHAYS, LUKE DAY, ADAM WHEELER " and ELI PARSONS," have enacted, " that rewards ad-" ditional to those offered and promised to be paid by the state " of Massachusetts Bay, for the apprehending the aforesaid " rebels, be offered by this state ;" WE do hereby offer the following rewards to any person or persons who shall, within the limits of this state, apprehend the rebels aforesaid, and secure them in the gaol of the city and county of Philadelphia, — viz. For the apprehending of the said Daniel Shays, and securing him as aforesaid, the reward of *One hundred and Fifty Pounds* lawful money of the state of Massachusetts Bay, and *One Hundred Pounds* lawful money of this state ; and for the apprehending the said Luke Day, Adam Wheeler and Eli Parsons, and securing them as aforesaid, the reward (respectively) of *One Hundred Pounds* lawful money of Massachusetts Bay and *Fifty Pounds* lawful money of this state : And all judges, justices, sheriffs and constables are hereby strictly enjoined and required to make diligent search and enquiry after, and to use their utmost endeavours to apprehend and secure the said Daniel Shays, Luke Day, Adam Wheeler and Eli Parsons, their aiders, abettors and comforters, and every of them, so that they may be dealt with according to law.

GIVEN in Council, under the hand of the President, and the Seal of the State, at Philadelphia, this tenth day of March, in the year of our Lord one thousand seven hundred and eighty-seven.

BENJAMIN FRANKLIN.

ATTEST

JOHN ARMSTRONG, jun. Secretary.

charged for their parts in the rebellion, but most of them were pardoned. Eighteen men were charged and received death sentences, but only two of the sentences were carried out. The two men who were executed had also committed other serious crimes.

The Ringleaders

The leaders of the rebellion had various fates. After fleeing from Petersham, Daniel Shays had escaped to Vermont, where he hid in the woods. In his absence, he was sentenced to death for **treason**. He was pardoned in 1788 after John Hancock was reelected governor of Massachusetts in May 1787.

Shays returned to Massachusetts and died in poverty in 1825. For his part in the rebellion, Luke Day was expelled from the **prestigious** Society of the Cincinnati, which counted George Washington and Alexander Hamilton as members. Job Shattuck had been in jail since his capture at Groton in 1786. In May 1787, he was put on trial for his part in the rebellion and sentenced to death. When John Hancock was reinstated as governor that same month, he pardoned Shattuck along with the other rebels.

John Hancock returned as governor of Massachusetts in 1787.

The Wider Impact

Shays' Rebellion led to widespread calls for the reform of the Articles of Confederation. Those who believed the rebellion had shown the weakness of the Articles of Confederation as a basis for government included George Washington.

THE FEDERALIST PAPERS

SHAYS' REBELLION TOOK PLACE DURING A DEBATE ABOUT THE SHAPE OF THE US GOVERNMENT. THOSE WHO WANTED TO LIMIT GOVERNMENT POWER WERE KNOWN AS ANTI-FEDERALISTS. THE CASE FOR STRONG GOVERNMENT WAS PUT IN A SERIES OF ARTICLES BETWEEN OCTOBER 1787 AND AUGUST 1788. THESE FEDERALIST PAPERS WERE THE WORK OF THE LEADING POLITICIANS ALEXANDER HAMILTON, JAMES MADISON, AND JOHN JAY.

The Federalist Papers were published under false names — but everyone knew the identity of the authors.

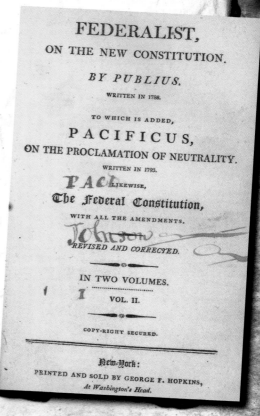

FEDERALIST,
ON THE NEW CONSTITUTION.

BY PUBLIUS.

WRITTEN IN 1788.

TO WHICH IS ADDED,

PACIFICUS,
ON THE PROCLAMATION OF NEUTRALITY.

WRITTEN IN 1793.

LIKEWISE,

The Federal Constitution,

WITH ALL THE AMENDMENTS.

REVISED AND CORRECTED.

IN TWO VOLUMES.

VOL. II.

COPY-RIGHT SECURED.

New-York:
PRINTED AND SOLD BY GEORGE F. HOPKINS,
At Washington's Head.

Washington had retired from public life after leading the colonies to success in the Revolutionary War, but had watched events in Massachusetts closely. Washington realized that only a stronger federal government could prevent similar rebellions from happening in the future.

The Philadelphia Convention

In response to the crisis in Massachusetts, representatives of all the states except Rhode Island met at the national capital, Philadelphia, in May 1787 to draw up a new constitution. For the next 3 1/2 months, the representatives debated the form the government of the United States should take.

VERMONT BECOMES A STATE

ONE UNFORESEEN CONSEQUENCE OF SHAYS' REBELLION WAS THAT VERMONT BECAME THE 14TH STATE. AT THE TIME OF THE REBELLION, VERMONT WAS AN INDEPENDENT REPUBLIC, AND THE REBEL LEADERS TOOK SHELTER THERE. ALEXANDER HAMILTON PUSHED FOR VERMONT TO BECOME A STATE. THAT WOULD ALLOW US FORCES TO CHASE ANY REBELS THERE IN THE FUTURE. AFTER LONG TALKS, VERMONT BECAME A STATE IN MARCH 1791.

Vermont is famous for its small towns and wooded hills.

Rather than simply changing the Articles of Confederation, it soon became clear that the Philadelphia Convention needed to come up with a plan that gave more power to the federal goverment. The delegates hoped to prevent any of the states becoming destabilized in the same way as Massachusetts had. They limited the power of individual states and at the same time gave the federal government more powers to intervene in the affairs of the states. The delegates at the convention agreed that the US Congress would have the power to suspend habeas corpus in the event of any rebellions in any of the states.

The US Constitution

On September 17, 1787, the delegates at the Philadelphia Convention finally agreed and signed the US Constitution. The document set up the framework for a federal government and the division of responsibilities between the national government and the states. It also guaranteed certain rights for all its citizens. A few years later, in 1791, the Bill of Rights added to those rights.

Some delegates in Philadelphia were worried that Massachusetts would refuse to **ratify** the US Constitution, but their worries were unfounded. When the vote was taken in Massachusetts on February 6, 1788, the Constitution was passed by 187 to 168 votes. The Constitution was finally ratified on June 21, 1788.

Another Consequence

An indirect outcome of Shays' Rebellion was that George Washington became the first president of the United States. The rebellion had convinced Washington to reenter political life. He agreed to chair the Philadelphia Convention, and his presence made people take seriously the efforts to create a new constitution and to accept its authority.

→

The delegates debated the Constitution in Independence Hall in Philadelphia.

GEORGE WASHINGTON

GEORGE WASHINGTON (1732–1799) HAD BECOME AN AMERICAN HERO AFTER LEADING THE CONTINENTAL ARMY TO VICTORY IN THE REVOLUTIONARY WAR. HE HAD RETIRED AT THE END OF THE WAR, BUT AGREED TO SERVE AS PRESIDENT AT THE CONVENTION IN PHILADELPHIA. WASHINGTON'S NAME WAS THE FIRST SIGNATURE ON THE US CONSTITUTION. HE SERVED AS THE FIRST PRESIDENT OF THE UNITED STATES, HOLDING OFFICE FROM 1789 UNTIL 1797. HE REMAINS ONE OF THE MOST REVERED OF ALL US PRESIDENTS.

The constitution called for a president to take charge of the federal government. Washington's fellow attendees voted him to be the first president. Washington took the oath of office on April 30, 1789.

George Washington was a successful farmer from Mount Vernon, Virginia.

The US Constitution was signed on September 17, 1787.

How Significant Was the Rebellion?

Historians still debate the impact of Shays' Rebellion on the United States. It persuaded senior political leaders such as George Washington and Alexander Hamilton of the need to strengthen the national government. Those with such views became known as Federalists. They were opposed by the anti-Federalists, who were wary of giving too much power to a centralized government. Arguments about federal rights versus states' rights eventually led to the Civil War (1861–1865), when Southern states went to war over their right to ignore federal laws. Arguments about the limits of national government continue today.

TIMELINE

1781 **October 19:** American forces defeat the British at the Battle of Yorktown, ending the fighting in the Revolutionary War.

1783 **September 3:** The British and the United States sign the Treaty of Paris, formally ending the war.

November: A slowdown in trade after the peace treaty begins a severe recession in the United States.

1784 **October:** The United States is in a critical economic crisis.

1785 **May:** John Hancock is replaced as governor of Massachusetts by James Bowdoin.

1786 **August 29:** Daniel Shays leads a group of rebels to Northampton to prevent the court from sitting there.

September 2: Governor Bowdoin issues a proclamation condemning the rebels as a "mob."

September 5: The rebels prevent the court sitting in Worcester County.

September 11: Eleven leaders of the rebels appear in court.

September 26: The government of Massachusetts summons volunteers to protect the courthouse in Springfield. After a standoff, rebels claim control of the courthouse.

October: The Massachusetts government introduces a riot act to give the militia more control to defeat the rebels.

November: Job Shattuck is arrested in Groton for his role in the disturbances.

1787 **January 19:** General Benjamin Lincoln leads his militia force west to face the rebels.

January 25: On a snowy day, two columns of rebels attack militia defending the Springfield Arsenal. They are easily defeated and flee.

February 3–4: After an overnight march, Lincoln surprises the rebels in their camp at Petersham. He claims to capture 150 Regulators. The others flee.

February 27: Around 120 rebels make a final attack at Stockbridge but are fought off by local militia.

May: John Hancock returns as governor of Massachusetts. He pardons Job Shattuck who has been sentenced to death. Delegates from the US states meet in Philadelphia to draft a new national constitution.

September 17: The US Constitution is signed in Philadelphia. George Washington's is the first signature.

1788 **February 6:** The Massachusetts government approves the Constitution.

June 21: The Constitution is ratified and becomes law.

1789 **April 30:** George Washington takes the oath as the first US president.

GLOSSARY

allegiance: Loyalty to a group or cause.

alliances: Formal agreements to work together for a certain purpose.

armory: A place where weapons are made.

arsenal: A collection of weapons and ammunition.

back salaries: Money people have earned that has not been paid.

bankrupt: Describes someone who cannot pay his or her debts.

boom: A period of intense economic activity.

centralized: Brought under a single authority.

colonies: Regions that are governed by other countries.

debtors: People who owe money.

disowned: No longer acknowledged by one's family.

excitable: Responding too easily to things in an unpredictable way.

forced march: A fast march without rest over a long distance.

grievances: Complaints.

habeas corpus: A law that people who are arrested must appear before a court.

imported: Describes goods brought into a country for sale.

indicted: Formally accused of a crime.

inflation: A period of a general rise in prices.

militia: Citizens who act as an armed force in an emergency.

petitions: Formal written requests to the authorities about an issue.

prestigious: Inspiring admiration and respect.

proclamation: An official announcement about an important subject.

ratify: To give formal approval to a proposal.

recession: A period of declining economic activity.

regime: A system for doing things.

republic: A state governed by the representatives of its people.

ringleaders: People who begin and lead unlawful activity.

smallholders: People who run small farms.

symbolic: Standing for or representing something else.

treason: The crime of betraying one's country.

FURTHER INFORMATION

Books

Burgan, Michael.
Shays' Rebellion. We the People: Revolution and the New Nation. Minneapolis, Minn: Compass Point Books, 2008.

Hull, Mary E.
Shays' Rebellion and the Constitution in American History. Berkeley Heights, NJ: Enslow Publlishers, 2000.

Somerville, Barbara A.
John Hancock: Signer for Independence. Signature Lives: Revolutionary War Era. Minneapolis, Minn: Compass Point Books, 2005.

Wolfe, James, and Heather Moehn.
Understanding the US Constitution. Primary Sources of American Political Documents. Berkeley Heights, NJ: Enslow Publishers, 2015.

Websites

www.government-and -constitution.org/history -us-political-parties/shays -rebellion.htm
An overview of the place of Shays' Rebellion in US political history.

kidskonnect.com/history/ shays-rebellion/
A downloadable study sheet about the rebellion and its effects.

www.history.com/topics/ shays-rebellion
An overview of the rebellion, with links to associated videos.

www.watchknowlearn.org/
Type Shays' Rebellion into the search box to watch a 6-minute video about the rebellion.

INDEX

Amherst 34
Articles of Confederation 8, 10, 38, 40
Ashley, John 35

banknotes 11, 14, 22
Bill of Rights 41
Boston 6, 14, 27
Bowdoin, John 9, 11, 12, 15, 20, 27, 28, 30
British Parliament Act 6

Civil War 43
coinage, gold and silver 8, 9
colonies, British 4, 5, 6, 8, 9, 10
Concord Courthouse 18
Congress, US 10, 11, 30
Constitution, US 37, 41, 42
Continental Army 5, 21, 28, 30, 42
Continental currency 14

Day, Luke 16, 17, 21, 27, 30, 31, 38
debts, personal 8, 12, 16, 22

economy 6, 7, 10

Federalists 39, 43
Franklin, Benjamin 36

Groton 17, 19, 25, 38

habeas corpus 24, 25, 40
Hamilton, Alexander 38, 39, 40, 43
Hancock, John 8, 9, 14, 37, 29

Lincoln, Benjamin 28, 29, 34, 35

militia 22, 23, 26, 27, 30, 35
money 8, 9, 11, 14, 22

North Carolina 17
Northampton courthouse 15, 20

Parsons, Eli 30, 32
Petersham 34, 36
Philadelphia Convention 39–41

Regulators 17, 18, 20, 21, 22, 23, 25, 27, 28, 29, 30, 35
Revolutionary War 4, 6, 9, 12, 13, 14, 16, 18, 39, 42
Rhode Island 22
Riot Act 24, 26

Saratoga, Battle of 16
Shattuck, Job 13, 17, 18, 19, 25, 27, 38
Shays, Daniel 13, 14, 15, 17, 21, 23, 27, 30, 31, 32, 33, 34, 37, 38
Shepard, General William 21, 23, 29, 30, 32
Springfield 6, 21, 22, 23, 24, 29, 30–33
Stiles, Ezra 35
Stockbridge 35

taxation 7, 11, 17, 19, 22

Vermont 34, 37, 40

Washington, George 28, 32, 38, 39, 41, 42, 43
Worcester County 20, 21